THE GREAT
I AM IN
YOUR FATE

Charleston, SC
www.PalmettoPublishing.com

The Great I AM In Your Fate
Copyright © 2022 by L. Vesel

Paperback ISBN: 979-8-8229-0823-9

THE GREAT I AM IN YOUR FATE

The secret of your purpose and destiny
is in a strong foundation in the Lord.

L. VESEL

TABLE OF CONTENTS

INTRODUCTION

Who has put wisdom in the mind? Or who has given understanding to the heart?

—Job 38:36, NKJV

Truth calls to reason to discover meaning, and the knowledge of truth is wisdom.

Mankind has entered a new era of progress of digital, intellectual, and information technologies.

Knowledge is multiplied, and the race for global dominance and competition increases. The process has been launched and cannot be stopped.

The world system of government and domination depends on the ideological consciousness of those who rule and dominate, where truth is weighed on the scales of God on the one hand and corruption and lies on the other hand.

Every idea of humanity comes from the information received in the process of researching the existing reality and is a product of the mind and the fruit of the spirit.

An idea cannot be eliminated, but it is possible to reboot, or be renewed by, the spirit of the mind in the knowledge of the truth.

The original idea, as a product of the highest intellect and mind, is the idea of God's creation, where there is no place for competition.

In the idea of God's creation, there are purposes, foundations, assignments, applications, and results, and in the spirit of the idea, everything is already perfect and accomplished. God knows the result and proclaims from the beginning what will be in the end.

The material world, created by God, is the incorporation of his idea into visible matter since the visible came from the invisible.

God the Creator, as the supreme legislator, established his laws, standards, conditions, morality, times, and dates; only he has the right to qualify and judge in accordance with his law, provisions, and standards.

It is in his right to evaluate what is true and what is false in the very conception of an idea since every idea is born in the spirit. God is a Spirit who exists independently of the existing visible reality.

The product of the divine idea of creation as an attribute, I AM WHO I AM, and the fruit of his idea determine the significance as an attribute: WHO AM I. God is an absolute intellect, a mind in the power of vitality and spirituality, speaking the truth from within as a set of vital information.

He gives meaning to the mind and puts wisdom into the heart of anyone who wants to seek the truth and understand the meaning of life.

Believe in the True God and No Other

Chapter 1
Essence of Being

See, I have set before you today life and good, death and evil.
—Deuteronomy 30:15, NKJV

"To everything there is a season, A time for every purpose under heaven. A time to be born and a time to die." And the whole life of man is vanity of vanities, as the book of Ecclesiastes says in 3:1.

For everyone who was born and came into this world, there is a time and a beginning, and then a small interval of his path called life.

What lies ahead for him on this life path? Man does not know, and he does not know what his future is; is it good or bad?

As a man came out of the womb of his mother naked, so he departs as he came.

It does not matter where a person was born, in what corner of the vast globe, what nationality, what color of skin.

It doesn't matter whether a person was born on time or not on time. In times of peace or war or in times of abundance or poverty. In ancient times or in the present times of civilizations and progress.

Whether that fact suits the person—where, when, and how he was born and came into this world—one way or another, a person is given the opportunity to be born into this world and given the right to life.

And if the breath of life is given to him from God, then that is the will of God. With the first breath of air, with the first cry of a baby, time inexorably begins to count seconds, minutes, hours, days, and years.

Man is given a period of time in his place of dwelling on this earth. And this gap includes the process of growing a personality, realizing the reality of being; truth and deceit, good and evil, life and death take place in this gap.

Man is given the opportunity and ability to think and distinguish between good and evil, truth and falsehood. A person is given the right to choose in making decisions in the process of growth of an emerging personality.

A person is faced with the choices of life values and priorities, meaning upon what basis he lays his foundation as a person of will and character.

What will he choose as a basis in building his destiny, where there is essentially only one correct choice?

Man was given a body to do good deeds and not be an accomplice of evil, bringing pain, suffering, and death, and where there is death, there is no life.

What a person sows while living in the body, that he will reap, since every good is paid for with good, and every ill will and evil returns to that from whom it comes. Nobody canceled the law of sowing and reaping and gathering fruits, and this law is still in force today.

Everything that a person understands and does from the abundance of his heart is in the sight of God and people. And God knows the thoughts and heart intentions of everyone.

Therefore, as a man wants to be treated by people, so let him act accordingly. In the same way, God deals with the honest according to honesty and with the evil one according to the wickedness of man.

Here is what I have seen: It is good and fitting for one to eat and drink, and to enjoy the good of all his labor in which he toils under the sun all the days of his life which God gives him; for it is his heritage. As for every man to whom God has given riches and wealth, and given him power to eat of it, to receive his heritage and rejoice in his labor—this is the gift of God.

—Ecclesiastes 5:18–19, NKJV

The days of our lives are seventy years; And if by reason of strength they are eighty years, Yet their boast is only labor and sorrow; For it is soon cut off, and we fly away.

—Psalm 90:10, NKJV

In this small gap in the life path given by God to man, a deep meaning is hidden. With God the Creator, everything has meaning and significance.

Any person who wants to know the meaning of life, naturally, must turn to the one who discovers the meaning of the mind—that is, to the Creator, who created man.

Only God, who created man, knows what is in man—namely, his spirit, soul, and body. He knows how this body functions, both externally and internally.

God has given man instruction or commandment of unity, in which the free will of man must conform to the will of God. The key to achieving the set commandment of unity—that is, holiness— is obedience and due reverence to the one who gave the breath of life.

The foundation of trust is the desire (will) to abide in the love of God the Father and under his wise guidance to man—namely, vision and strategy of dominance on the planet Earth.

The heaven, even the heavens, are the LORD's; But the earth He has given to the children of men.

—Psalm 115:16, NKJV

Vision without awareness of value, and as a result without discipline, and awareness of value forms character, strong-willed character in obedience and fidelity.

With God, everything is in a certain order, which means for everyone there is a beginning—the period of infancy, then a period of search and choice, then a period that determines the fate of an accomplished personality.

It is not the beginning that determines the personality but the end, and winners are not born but become them.

The tragedy of humanity lies in the fact that humanity does not want to discipline itself based on the law of truth and follow the principles of the one God—the Creator, who was and is and abides forever, and there is no other.

The fear of the LORD is the beginning of wisdom, And the knowledge of the Holy One is understanding.

—Proverbs 9:10, NKJV

An intelligent person seeks the truth, and the more he learns about God's will to a person, the more he realizes the meaning of life. What is the essence of being?

And He has made from one blood every nation of men to dwell on all the face of the earth, and has determined their preappointed times and the boundaries

of their dwellings so that they should seek the Lord, in the hope that they might grope for Him and find Him, though He is not far from each one of us.
—Acts 17:26–27, NKJV

The choice of a person determines his fate, living in the body. A person either acquires or squanders, and the main essence is in approaching God in a conscious decision, controlling his emotions and feelings, and acquiring skills and experience in obedience and fidelity.

And vice versa: A person who has not learned self-control, ignoring the promptings of conscience, moves away from the presence of God in the wrong direction.

God gives life and vitality in this temporary earthly life. Naturally, vitality is impossible without a giver. Not in the power of a person, every breath of air and exhalation, but thanks to the Giver of breath.

God gave everyone who came into this world a privilege in a unique opportunity: first, to know that God exists; second, to know who he is; third, to know who man is and what the will of God is for man.

This is the whole meaning and foundation on which everyone who knows the will of God with all his mind and heart will be successful in building his destiny.

To believe in God is the decision of each individual person who has the ability to understand the reality of existence, the essence of being and what is the main meaning of the divine idea of creation. What is a person—his identity with which he identifies himself? If a person recognizes the divine idea of creation, then he also recognizes that he is a creation of God, created in the image of God and identical to that image from the very beginning in the idea of creation. In this case, the question arises: Where is the beginning of man, his source? Reflecting on this question comes the understanding that the source of existence is in the divine existence itself. Man exists because God is really existing. From this affirmation naturally comes understanding; God-given life to everyone who came into this world with a purpose, and everyone is given the potential to achieve this goal.

Faith in God is confidence in the invisible God on the one hand and the realization or construction of one's destiny, based on this statement in one's faith, in order to fulfill the will of God in anticipation of the promised, not yet visible but firmly convinced that God is the source and the perfecter of the faith of everyone who believes in him. The rejection of the existence of God is the fruit of ideological thinking, freeing one from any responsibility and giving freedom to philosophical sophistication. Recognition of God, the Creator and Legislator, obliges one to exercise discipline and responsibility.

CHAPTER 2
THE LAW OF CREATION—THE LAW OF TRUTH

Let them praise the name of the LORD, For He commanded and they were created. He also established them forever and ever; He made a decree which shall not pass away.

—Psalm 148:5–6, NKJV

Absolute truth has a firm and unshakable basis in the fact that God, even before the creation of the universe, was and is and remains forever in infinite space and outside the dimension of time.

God is an inexhaustible intellect, a mind incomprehensible to the human mind and invisible to the human eye "who alone has immortality, dwelling in unapproachable light, whom no man has seen or can see, to whom be honor and everlasting power" (1 Tim. 6:16, NKJV).

No one knows what is inside God; no one understands what is in God's thoughts: "'For My thoughts are not your thoughts, Nor are your ways My ways,' says the LORD" (Isa. 55:8, NKJV).

No one has ever seen God, and it is impossible to see God. God is Spirit, a mighty, ever-moving force, in infinite space: "And the Spirit of God was hovering over the face of the waters" (Gen 1:2, NKJV).

God is Spirit, and those who worship Him must worship in spirit and truth.
—John 4:24, NKJV

God is the breath of eternity: "The wind blows where it wishes, and you hear the sound of it, but cannot tell where it comes from and where it goes" (John 3:8, NKJV).

God is not limited by anything, in anything, anywhere, ever. God has freedom of thought, and God's idea of the creation of the universe is in God himself, in his bowels, in his mind, in his Spirit—within God.

And only God himself knows absolutely everything, in a certain order, from beginning to end—the whole process of creation.

God has neither beginning nor end, and in his idea, he decided to be the beginning (alpha) and the end (omega).

And the foundation of the beginning is the truth and righteousness of God. Truth is the divine thought of the ingenious plan of the creative process. God realized his thought, born in the Spirit of God's intellect, into reality. As written, out of the invisible came the visible.

On the basis of the truth of God—everything is arranged, and everything is subordinated under the authority of the power of the law of truth. God confirmed his truth and legitimized it, laying it in the foundation in the process of creation.

The truth is that God exists. He proclaimed his name—I AM—making it clear that there is no other. He is the originator of his idea of creation; he is the life-giving Spirit, giving life to all living things. Everything is contained by him, and everything was created by him and for him.

For by Him all things were created that are in heaven and that are on earth, visible and invisible, whether thrones or dominions or principalities or powers. All things were created through Him and for Him. And He is before all things, and in Him all things consist.

—Colossians 1:16–17, NKJV

He is the only one and is the supreme Legislator and Owner of everything that exists, both the invisible (spiritual) world and the visible (material) world and everything that fills them.

God as the Creator and legislator is also the supreme judge in space and time: "There is only one Lawgiver and Judge" (James 4:12, NIV).

Ages and dates in the process of creation have a starting point from alpha to omega, and the whole idea of God's creative process in time and space has a purpose and foundation.

God, as the supreme Legislator, established for everything he created his principles, regulations, standards, measurements, conditions, moral norms, and laws according to his will, according to the will of God the Creator and Father of all created creatures, the Father of every spirit and flesh and body.

How much more should we submit to the Father of spirits and live!

—Hebrews 12:9, NIV

O God, the God of the spirits of all flesh.

—Numbers 16:22, NKJV

*The hope of the gospel which you heard, which was preached to every crea-
ture under heaven.*

—Colossians 1:23, NKJV

*There are also heavenly bodies and there are earthly bodies; but the splendor
of the heavenly bodies is one kind, and the splendor of the earthly bodies
is another.*

—1 Corinthians 15:40, NIV

The principles of the law of creation require things created by
God, the visible (material) and invisible (spiritual) world and everything that fills them, to contain what is determined by God and
to function and cooperate according to God's laws and standards.

The laws of God are active and established in truth. And no
one and nothing, neither in heaven nor on earth, has the power
and authority to violate or change them. Anyone who opposes
God will not stand in his intentions.

It is a fearful thing to fall into the hands of the living God.

—Hebrews 10:31, NKJV

*All creation is contained by the mighty power of God's spoken word: God
spoke, and it was so.*

—Genesis 1:3, NKJV

In space, the planets, the sun, the moon, and the stars function according to God's design, with purpose and His law, to shine upon the Earth, to separate light from darkness, to separate day from night, and for signs and times and days and years.

—Genesis 1:14, NKJV

The Earth does not leave its orbit and rotates on its axis for the benefit of those who live on it. And the heavens are established by God's word.

—Genesis 1:1, NKJV

The waters gathered in their place and do not go beyond what is available. Every seed brings forth fruit after its kind.

—Genesis 1:11, NKJV

Every living soul produces according to its kind, both on earth and in water.

—Genesis 1:22, NKJV

And God created man in his own image, perfectly reflecting the image, in accordance with the ideal plan of creation; endowing him with the spirit of intellect; breathing into him the breath of life; placing this gift from God in the body and providing freedom of choice (will).

God gives mankind the rights and opportunities in his further self-development, subject to direct contact, at the level of the spirit, in unified harmony with the dignity of the reflecting Creator.

Just as all creation is contained by the power of the word of God, so is man, the creation of God, maintained by the same word and Spirit for the glory of God, reflecting the image of the Lord.

Humanity in the idea of the Creator, as the numerous heritages of God inhabiting the planet Earth, is the main priority in the fulfillment of the will of God.

Your kingdom come. Your will be done On earth as it is in heaven.
—Matthew 6:10, NKJV

God, who created a man and a woman, called them a man: "So God created man in His own image; in the image of God He created him; male and female He created them" (Gen. 1:27, NKJV). Not only a man but also a woman, putting into it the meaning and significance not only in the physical sphere but also in the spiritual sense.

Then God blessed them, and God said to them, "Be fruitful and multiply; fill the earth and subdue it; have dominion over the fish of the sea, over the birds of the air, and over every living thing that moves on the earth."
—Genesis 1:28, NKJV

Mankind, as a royal priesthood for the glory of God, was created by him for good deeds, with God-given authority and power, with the aim of representing the heavenly kingdom on earth, placing all responsibility in accordance with the standards established by him.

God approved the law of reproduction for the purpose of constant renewal, giving man the basis of reasonable domination (administrative management) and blessed them: (1) produce (be fruitful); (2) multiply (reproduce); (3) distribute (fill and inherit the earth); (4) manage (order); and (5) bear responsibility (dominate).

And this, too, is the basis of any business.

The Creator entrusted man with the planet—the earth, with all its inhabitants (animal and plant life).

Everything that a person will produce and create, improving in all knowledge, must comply with the established standard: God giving and mankind receiving, consuming, and acquiring blessings in abundance.

The whole meaning lies in the commandment of unity between man and God. Unity in spirit (the intellectual mind) and in truth (the will of man is subordinate to the will of God) is holiness, without which the presence of God is not possible, and the result of holiness is eternal life, or abiding, the opposite of death (Rom. 6:22, NKJV).

Essentially, the kingdom of God begins with each and every person: "For indeed, the kingdom of God is within you" (Luke 17:21, NKJV). Unity in spirit and truth is holiness.

The thought and idea of the kingdom are traced through all scripture; as the King is, so is the kingdom.

Throughout the Old Testament, every king who had the fear of God as a person was successful during his reign, and vice versa. What God wants to show like examples of worthy and unworthy, faithful and unfaithful, truthful and hypocritical, fulfilling the will of God or rejecting it.

The main priority in the idea of the creation of man is not a competing personality but a dominant personality, as a pillar and affirmation of the truth.

God revealed himself to man as a loving Father to his children, setting the standard of relationships in the example of the family, where children through obedience achieve the dignity and honor of the title and inheritance and parents, in turn, through obedience to God and the Father, also achieve the dignity of being called children of God and heirs.

A society consisting of families that are morally stable, affirmed in the truth, and having the fear of God is the guarantor of the well-being of the state.

The foundation of any state is the law and the constitution in the current parameters of power, including legislative, executive, and judicial. The strength of any state, stability, and sovereignty is in existing laws and law-abiding citizens: "Where there is no revelation, people cast off restraint; but blessed is the one who heeds wisdom's instruction" (Prov. 29:18, NIV).

Revelation from God is given to law-abiding men who fulfill the will of God and are established on the divine principles of righteousness, hence the moral and cultural state and historical consciousness of any nation.

The principles of legal provisions determine the ideological essence, morality, and moral value.

People change laws and make amendments for the sake of the moral state of nations, going against the divine principles of truth and righteousness, which entails a catastrophic and inevitable consequence—which is observed at the present time, as well as repeating but accelerating in time and space.

The information war is built on lies, introducing ideas that destroy moral value in the minds of the new generation. This is what gives rise to licentiousness, lack of control, unbridled behavior, and lawlessness.

But God is not a man to be changed by someone or something. Our sovereign God cannot resist Himself: "God is not human, that he should lie, not a human being, that he should change his mind. Does he speak and then not act? Does he promise and not fulfill?" (Num. 23:19, NIV).

God is faithful to his principles in the implementation of his ideas, and no one and nothing has the power and authority to compete with God and oppose the law of truth.

Ideas that reject truth are ultimately destructive and catastrophic.

Truth appeals to reason to this day; stop in perseverance, and obey the law of truth in order to live: "Forsake foolishness and live, And go in the way of understanding" (Prov. 9:6, NKJV).

Man is changeable, deceitful, and fickle in his sinful nature, but God is holy, one and faithful. He has power and authority: "God is light and in Him is no darkness at all" (1 John 1:5, NKJV).

Holy or *holiness* has the meaning of "one whole in fullness."

God exists as one in fullness (only).

He is the Spirit of reason and the highest intellect in uniqueness and beyond accuracy in ingenuity and creation of the universe. He has vitality in himself and gives life to all living things. He is the one who speaks the word, who speaks the truth from within.

The law of creation is the law of the truth of God, approved by God himself—the Creator in the legislative power, acting in executive and judicial power. But the mercy of God is a gift of grace—in the justifying power given by God the Creator in his Son, who is the word of God.

Remember the former things of old, For I am God, and there is no other; I am God, and there is none like Me. Declaring the end from the beginning, And from ancient times things that are not yet done, Saying, "My counsel shall stand, And I will do all My pleasure."

—Isaiah 46:9–10, NKJV

The work of righteousness will be peace, And the effect of righteousness, quietness and assurance forever.

—Isaiah 32:17, NKJV

The law of creation is based on a fundamental basis—on truth, and the truth is the self-affirmation of this basis, which is God himself, the Creator. He is the primary source of everything that exists, and the law of truth lies in the fact that only in one God—the Creator in the aggregate is the whole law, all standards, and only he is the only Legislator and Judge and Human Rights Activist.

The idea of the existence of other gods is the result of thinking based on information. God the Creator is the source of true information, while the information coming from the sources as a result of the study of the existing reality is already a system of conceptually formed thoughts and is a prototype of the original idea that goes against the idea of the Creator.

CHAPTER 3
REJECTING THE IDEA OF GOD— CRAZY DELUSION

The idea of God the Creator is crowned with truth, and anyone who rejects God's truth is guilty of crazy delusion.

Ideology is the scientific substantiation of any thought; it is a set of thinking expressed in a word. Every idea includes five aspects: purpose, foundation, assignments, application, and result.

The primordial idea, as a product of the highest intellect and mind, is the idea of God's creation of the universe, where God is the Creator and Founder.

Every idea is born in the spirit. God is Spirit, and his idea was born in his Spirit of intellect in him. And only he has the power to develop his idea, which is fundamental in every sense.

Every idea develops in the mind. God, at the highest level of the intellectual mind, developed the idea, calculating impeccable perfection to superaccuracy, laying the foundation for the ideal of the stability of truth.

Every idea in its development is realized in implementation. An unspoken idea remains an idea inside; an idea expressed in a word characterizes a person—that is, what kind of spirit he is.

The first word was not spoken by man but by God. God spoke and happened in reality, and reality itself characterizes the Creator, who creates in the Spirit of vitality and spirituality.

An ideology is a prototype of the primordial idea, and this is no longer the original but a system of conceptually formulated thoughts. The word concept means "the birth of thought in the intellectual spirit."

Any such ideological system has a place of implementation, but the result is ultimately qualified by God's standard.

God determined in his idea the beginning and the end in space and time, and in this interval from alpha to omega, there is definitely a purpose and meaning, until the moment when God realizes the new. No one knows when and how, but one thing is clear: that everything God intended will happen exactly as it was intended in the ideal plan of creation.

In the beginning God created the heavens and the earth.
—Genesis 1:1, NKJV

Then He who sat on the throne said, "Behold, I make all things new."
—Revelation 21:5, NKJV

God's idea is based on an uncompromising conceptual truth and cannot be disputed, and in an ideological system, disputes are possible arguments, justifying or compromising, since God provided the possibility of freedom of thought.

Therefore, any idea that came from the side of creation as a prototype contains a peculiar meaning or goal for strengthening and well-being in the development of creation, both in the spiritual sphere and in the material one, or it has negative consequences. In the worst case, it prevails with a destructive force against the divine idea.

The idea of a cherub—Lucifer—was exposed by God from within, at the moment of generation in the spirit before the development of this plan. The result of the idea of apostasy is condemnation, according to the law of creation. Lucifer was stripped of all powers of dignity and banished from the presence of God. In exile, he is that spirit of apostasy, wandering and restless.

God the Creator, as the ancestor of the idea of creation, is the Father who gives life and is also the Father of every spirit: angels, seraphim, archangels, cherubim, and the entire heavenly host in the invisible spiritual world.

The idea of apostasy is expressed in the word: "I will ascend above the heights of the clouds, I will be like the Most High" (Isa. 14:14, NKJV). The idea of self-important superiority is pride.

The same spirit of pride is now at work in the sons of disobedience in the wandering thoughts of mankind.

So it was in ancient times, when those who ruled and dominated imagined themselves to be gods, deluded in their reasoning, rejecting the will of God. Their fall was determined by God in the end.

In the same way, the spirit of error is at work in the present times, replacing the truth with a lie, distorting the word of God, erring and misleading the unconfirmed and uncertain in their thinking: "But evil men and impostors will grow worse and worse, deceiving and being deceived" (2 Tim. 3:13, NKJV).

The same spirit that rebels against the truth influences thinking in a subtle and corrupt way, giving rise to a philosophical ideology.

Beware lest anyone cheat you through philosophy and empty deceit, according to the tradition of men, according to the basic principles of the world, and not according to Christ.

—Colossians 2:8, NKJV

Comparing someone or something to God is worse than replacing God and his truth. This is the main meaning of the philosophical ideology of apostates from the truth: "Make us gods that shall go before us" (Ex. 32:1, NKJV).

And they worshiped the beast, saying, "Who is like the beast? Who is able to make war with him?"

—Revelation 13:4, NKJV

In the original, the word *philosophy* from the Greek means "love" (*phillo*) and "wisdom" (*sophios*). Philosophy is a special form of knowledge of the universe, which develops a system of knowledge. Philosophy is a way of influencing thinking and is a product of an idea, and an idea is a product of thinking.

Ultimately, the result determines the entire philosophy of ideological thinking. The type of spirit of thinking one uses—such the heart's intentions, desires, goals, plans, and actions—entails consequences. It can be beneficial and pleasing to God or not.

Actions turn into habits and traditions, defining personality.

When a person thinks, he is who he is inside himself. But when he expresses his thoughts aloud, then he becomes someone who characterizes his individuality or his inner spiritual state.

An idea has the risk of being erroneous; then the whole philosophy of human life will proceed in the wrong direction, away from God.

In the idea of God, philosophy is love for creation and love for man, and the philosophy of human life is mutual love for God, in order to correspond to the dignity of being and being called children of God.

A son honors his father, And a servant his master. If then I am the Father, Where is My honor? And if I am a Master, Where is My reverence? Says the LORD of hosts.

—Malachi 1:6, NKJV

Parents are worthy of honor and respect in this temporary earthly life. The Lord is a God worthy of reverence in purity of righteousness and holiness. God is holy and desires that his children, living in this temporary earthly life, be admonished by him, his Holy Spirit, and not succumb to the influence of the spirit of apostasy.

For this reason, God, invisible to the human eye, provided a person with a unique opportunity to take his place as a person who is in the will of God, and his will is in his word.

God visually provided his word, as it is provided in the original, in accordance with the law of truth, where God is everything and in everything, primarily for man.

The guarantor of purity and righteousness in communion with God is the unity of Spirit and truth, which means the word of God is the law for a person, as a lifestyle and as the main priority in building his destiny. A person who knows the truth abides in God, guided by revelations from God.

And if an obedient son honors his father by his obedience, then he who honors God and the Lord of lords honors him in his fidelity and love, and love is the totality of perfection, which is poured into our hearts by the Holy Spirit.

Without revelation from above, the people are unbridled, but those who have knowledge from the Lord are successful in everything. A person who has skills and experience in communicating with God grows spiritually. He who has proven the authority of fidelity and stability is the ideal in the divine idea of creating a person as worshiping God in spirit and truth.

But the hour is coming, and now is, when the true worshipers will worship the Father in spirit and truth; for the Father is seeking such to worship Him. God is Spirit, and those who worship Him must worship in spirit and truth.

—John 4:23–24, NKJV

The will of man corresponds to the will of God, and the will of God is in keeping with the commandment and the law of righteousness to the sanctification of man before God. And this is the whole point of the law of righteousness, without adding anything or subtracting anything, but keeping exactly this law of righteousness: "and if anyone takes away from the words of the book of this prophecy, God shall take away his part from the Book of Life" (Rev. 22:19). The book of life is with God the Father, in which the lives of each individual are inscribed, and all the deeds done in the body are recorded.

There is a danger in distorting of the word of God, forming all kinds of doctrines and religions, creating teachings about God, purely by philosophical means.

Philosophical theology distracts people from the content of divine revelation by suggesting theories and ideas, deifying creation (created by God), or deifying persons (created by God).

And changed the glory of the incorruptible God into an image made like corruptible man—and birds and four-footed animals and creeping things. Therefore God also gave them up to uncleanness, in the lusts of their hearts, to dishonor their bodies among themselves.

—Romans 1:23–24, NKJV

By creating myths and legends about other worlds and about the gods descended from heaven, thereby subordinating followers, the same erring ones, to the performance of rites, rituals, and traditions that determine their significance: "You shall have no other gods before Me" (Ex. 20:3, NKJV).

Theology is the totality of the doctrines of any religion. The word *religion* comes from the Latin *religare*, meaning "to bind, unite." This is a definite and strong system of beliefs and is an embedded idea with a philosophical bias in the doctrine of God.

And if in any of these teachings about God there are deviations from the original idea of God the Creator, then the whole religion of human life will be just a religious rite, a tradition that has no meaning in God's plan.

In the original, the word *theology* from Greek means "God" (*theo*) and "word" (*logos*), in the sense of knowing God and his truth. God, as a combination of vital information and wisdom, has the right to give a revelation of his truth for the purpose of instructing and admonishing in righteousness, but the key to receiving revelation from God is obedience and diligence.

In a real and sincere relationship with God, there is no place for philosophies, tensions, and self-will. God has shown his love for man by showing it in action on his part, but man has a choice to know that God exists, to know who he is, to know who man is, and to know what the will of God is for man. Then, man must naturally know, accept, and appreciate and then carry out in patience, obedience, humility, and dignity the life path given by God.

The main goal in God's plan is the rebirth of man (who is fallen, as a result of his disobedience). And for this, God provided everything possible for life and godliness.

The first man created by God had the ability to hear and obey; such a natural quality was endowed with man created by God. God endowed man with a will, giving freedom of choice. As a free-thinking being and aware of reality, a person was tested by God in the test of self-will. Man did not stand this test, but God, knowing this in advance, foresaw a solution to this conflict even before the creation of the world.

The first man neglected his original freedom in natural communion with the Father, choosing independence, but now everyone who wants to acquire this freedom in communion with God must achieve this right and dignity through obedience to the truth, and there is no other way.

Mankind, in the person of the first man—Adam—chose independence from God, so the last heritage of God restores mankind's trust and authority in complete harmony under the guidance of the Holy Spirit.

All cults and religions that deny the idea of God and the Creator, Elohim, and his truth, which appeared in the real material world, for the salvation, redemption, restoration, and rebirth of a fallen person, are driven by the spirit of the antichrist; suggestive ideas and theories of delusion are the path to madness.

The same spirit of apostasy seduced the first man, instilling the thought of doubt and temptation on that unfortunate day, the day of independence from God. The same wandering spirit, having no place of rest in time and space, rejected by God, seeks shelter through seducing and tempting and mastering the minds of mankind, replacing the truth with a lie.

Therefore do not let sin reign in your mortal body, that you should obey it in its lusts. And do not present your members as instruments of unrighteousness to sin, but present yourselves to God as being alive from the dead, and your members as instruments of righteousness to God. For sin shall not have dominion over you.

—Romans 6:12–14, NKJV

For the wages of sin is death, but the gift of God is eternal life in Christ Jesus our Lord.

—Romans 6:23, NKJV

The word *reasonable* comes from the word *reason*, and *insane* means "having no reason." There is a difference in "having" and "not having": having the firmness of the spirit of truth, capable of withstanding all temptations, or not having in himself that which is called "reason" to discern spirits and not be caught in the trap of the obstacle of madness into slavery to sin. Freedom is in the knowledge of truth.

Knowing God in Personal Relationship with Him

CHAPTER 4
THE WORD OF GOD

In the beginning was the Word, and the Word was with God, and the Word was God.

—John 1:1, NKJV

The first word was spoken by God, not by man. First has the meaning of "primacy, superiority, and independence." The first one who speaks from within, from the depths, from the center of presence and being itself, regardless of place and time: God spoke the word to the realization of being visible from invisible.

God in Himself, in his intellectual Spirit (as in a computer) foresaw and calculated everything with superaccuracy, having perfectly approved all the laws of mathematics, physics, chemistry, and gravity. Absolutely everything was planned by the Creator before the word was spoken: "In the beginning God created the heavens and the earth" (Gen. 1:1, NKJV). This is the moment when God's idea was born in his intellectual Spirit.

In the beginning he created—that is, before everything began to be, God was, and his word was in him, and his direct participation, presence, and very investment in this project is a guaranteeing obligation in himself.

Therefore, the leading and central role in his plan is occupied by himself: the Creator is the Father of everything created by him. The investment itself is expensive, in terms of the volume of fullness and the presence of his Spirit: sacrificial love. He knew in advance that creation would not stand the test of faithfulness. The first apostasy took place in the realm of the spirit, and God, knowing this, foresaw this.

The invisible God, before the creation of the universe, foresaw in advance as a Legislator and Lawyer, Judge and Defender, where mercy is exalted over judgment in the expiatory sacrifice of love revealed by him.

In the legislature for the violation of the law established by the Creator is condemnation according to the law. The expiatory, or paid price for a crime, is the compensation for what was lost as a result of the crime against the law.

The law says the wages of sin is death, but the gift of God is life abiding. Therefore, only God himself, who is the only one who has abiding life in himself, has placed all responsibility upon himself.

To condemn the law of sin and death, one must provide a justifying status without sin and vice as evidence to triumph over the law of condemnation—the law of justification to abiding life.

At the moment of God's spoken word—*"Let there be light"*; and *there was light."* (Gen. 1:3, NKJV) —His word entered into action. His word is the law, and not only this, but his word is also not just a substantive but is an active force in the life-giving Spirit. The word of God is in the power of the Spirit of God, in inextricable connection, containing vitality: "So shall My word be that goes forth from My mouth; It shall not return to Me void, But it shall accomplish what I please, And it shall prosper in the thing for which I sent it" (Isa. 55:11, NKJV).

The word of God is like a seed containing life in itself. When this seed falls into the environment, growing brings forth fruit pleasing to God. And this fruit belongs to him who sowed his seed—the word of God, which bears much fruit: "For He whom God has sent speaks the words of God, for God does not give the Spirit by measure" (John 3:34, NKJV).

Thus, in this seed is the life-giving Spirit. The Spirit of God, before the creation of the universe, engendered in himself, in his intellectual Spirit, stability, or an ideal that characterizes Himself. God is love (agape) as an action of his will in sacrificial love in the form of a Lamb prepared for the fulfillment and accomplishment of the will of the Father and the Creator.

As any seed that has an outer shell but contains life in itself is sown in the soil, so God extracted this seed of life from himself in order to fulfill what he pleases; namely, his essence justifies himself. He is the Judge, and he is the Protector. In him is justification for everyone who by faith receives this seed of life.

God is a Spirit, and in his Spirit, at the moment of the birth of the idea of creation, the conceptual, fundamental component—God's thought in the intellectual Spirit—was first of all created.

Before everything was created, God in his intellectual Spirit gave birth to the Firstborn—the Son. He is the Seed, the word of God in the power of the life-giving Spirit. He is the Lamb slain before the creation of the world in the intellectual Spirit of God.

God realized the embodiment of his idea by the power of the life-giving Spirit, first of all in the spiritual world in the spiritual sphere: "Thus the heavens and the earth, and all the host of them, were finished" (Gen. 2:1, NKJV). And this means that the one born in the intellectual Spirit of God is the Firstborn, a full-fledged master and Lord God: "When He again brings the firstborn into the world, He says: "Let all the angels of God worship Him" [transferring all powers and authority] (Heb. 1:6, NKJV).

You, LORD, in the beginning laid the foundation of the earth, And the heavens are the work of Your hands.

—Hebrews 1:10, NKJV

This is the history of the heavens and the earth when they were created, in the day that the LORD God made the earth and the heavens.

—Genesis 2:4, NKJV

The LORD by wisdom founded the earth; By understanding He established the heavens.

—Proverbs 3:19, NKJV

In God's intellectual mind and Spirit of ownership, the dignity of the title of the trinity was established by God himself in himself. God is the Father, God is the Son, and God is the Holy Spirit.

God the Creator—Elohim—created the intellectual spirit of the mind as the process of conception of the idea of creating the universe, but it was accomplished or brought into reality by the power of the life-giving Spirit emanating from him; that is, the process of bestowal from him is a fact of birth, as the fruit of his idea. The fruit of the idea of the Creator is the similarity of his intellectual mind. In other words, God gave birth to the beginning—the Firstborn—and gave Him a name that means "who is, who is from the beginning": the Lord God Jehovah (Ex. 3:14, NKJV). The Lord God Jehovah is the Lord of everything, both in the spiritual (invisible) world and in the physical, material (visible) world.

He exists from the beginning (alpha and omega). He is the fruit of divine love, born before any creature: "He is the image of the invisible God, the firstborn over all creation" (Col. 1:15, NKJV).

He was clothed with a robe dipped in blood, and His name is called The Word of God. And the armies in heaven, clothed in fine linen, white and clean, followed Him on white horses. And in the sixteenth verse it is written;

"And He has on His robe and on His thigh a name written:
KING OF KINGS AND LORD OF LORDS."

—Revelation 19:13–14, 16, NKJV

In the idea of the intellectual Spirit of God the Creator—
Elohim—everything is already done. The Lord God Jehovah proclaims from the beginning what will happen in the end; He is
the wisdom of God, He is Alpha and Omega, the beginning and
the end.

"I am the Alpha and the Omega, the Beginning and the End," says the Lord,
"who is and who was and who is to come, the Almighty."

—Revelation 1:8, NKJV

The Lord God Jehovah (YAHWEH) is in the spiritual world,
invisible to the human eye. But in the material world, people di-
rectly experience contact with a powerful manifestation of the
divine power, which influences and acts in their lives to elicit reverence and reverence for the Almighty God.

In accordance with the manifestation of divine power, people
have placed special significance in the name of Jehovah.

Genesis 15:2: Jehovah: Sovereign Lord, Lord, Adonai
Isaiah 1:24: Jehovah of Sabaoth: Mighty Israel, Jehovah, Sabaoth
Isaiah 40:28: Jehovah: Eternal God
Genesis 14:19: Jehovah, God most high: Lord of heaven
and Earth
Genesis 17:1: Jehovah, God Almighty: God Almighty
Genesis 22:15: Jehovah the Provider: Jehovah Jireh

Exodus 15:26: Jehovah the Healer: Jehovah Rapha
Exodus 17:15: Jehovah the Conqueror: Jehovah Nissi
Psalm 23:1: Jehovah the Shepherd: Jehovah Rohi
Judges 6:24: Jehovah is peace: Jehovah Shalom
Ezekiel 48:35: Jehovah: the Lord is there, God dwells in us

Do you not know that you are the temple of God and that the Spirit of God dwells in you?

—1 Corinthians 3:16, NKJV

The Lord God Jehovah was with the people of God, making covenants, giving laws in order to restore the relationship between God and man, and putting the meaning of the sacrament in the atoning sacrifice of love, where the key role is this principle: "FI will deliver this people from the power of the grave; I will redeem them from death. Where, O death, are your plagues? Where, O grave, is your destruction?" (Hosea 13:14, NIV).

The Lord God Jehovah who sanctifies and justifies the chosen people, whom he brought out of the bondage of Egypt, is called Jehovah Mekaddishkem or Jehovah Tsidkenu—the Lord who sanctifies, or the Lord our righteousness. This is the Lord personally illuminating each individual, justifying personally each one who receives this seed of life into abiding life and delivers himself from the power of hell; where sin is the sting of death, and death is the result of condemnation to sinful slavery.

The understanding of this truth frees everyone who is burdened with sinful slavery from all dependence, renewing their thinking with the Holy Spirit and giving birth from the word of God and from the Holy Spirit.

Elohim, "In the beginning God..." (Gen. 1:1, NKJV), is the Creator in the intellectual world of the divine consciousness, and the fruit of His consciousness is the realizing divine essence—the Lord God Jehovah (self-existent one) in the Spirit. Then in the material, visible world, the divine essence is revealed in the physical human body.

Born before the creation of the world into the spiritual world, the fruit of love, which existed from the beginning, was born in a human body into the material world: "For to us a child is born, to us a son is given, and the government will be on his shoulders. And he will be called Wonderful Counselor, Mighty God, Everlasting Father, Prince of Peace" (Isa. 9:6, NIV).

The baby was born in the body, and the Son given from above is the Firstborn and the beginning of beginnings, which is the mighty God, the Father of eternity, the life-giving Spirit, incarnated in the body of the baby. The same life-giving Spirit who breathed the breath of life into the created Adam, the same Spirit of eternity, was embodied in the baby in the womb of the mother of Mary, who gave birth to Jesus Christ: "Behold, the virgin shall conceive and bear a Son, and shall call His name Immanuel" (Isa. 7:14 NKJV).

Joseph, son of David, do not be afraid to take Mary home as your wife, because what is conceived in her is from the Holy Spirit. She will give birth to a son, and you are to give him the name Jesus, because he will save his people from their sins.

—Matthew 1:20–21, NIV

In the beginning was the Word, and the Word was with God, and the Word was God. He was in the beginning with God. All things were made through Him, and without Him nothing was made that was made. In Him was life, and the life was the light of men.

—John 1:1–4, NKJV

And the Word became flesh and dwelt among us, and we beheld His glory, the glory as of the only begotten of the Father, full of grace and truth.

—John 1:14, NKJV

The meaning of "one kinship" is the unity reflecting the divine essence of the Son in the Father and the Father in the Son: "Then they said to Him, 'Who are You?' And Jesus said to them, "Just what I have been saying to you from the beginning" (John 8:25, NKJV). Jehovah, the name that was testified on Mount Horeb of God before Moses, was also testified during the time of Jesus Christ's sojourn on earth before a multitude of people.

Jehovah who is—"I AM THAT I AM" (Ex. 3:14, KJV)—testified about himself, about his divine essence of being in an earthly body on Earth.

- "I am the bread of life. He who comes to Me shall never hunger, and he who believes in Me shall never thirst" (John 6:35, NKJV).

- "I am the light of the world. He who follows Me shall not walk in darkness, but have the light of life" (John 8:12, NKJV).

- "I am the door. If anyone enters by Me, he will be saved" (John 10:9, NKJV).

- "I am the good shepherd. The good shepherd gives His life for the sheep" (John 10:11, NKJV).

- "I am the resurrection and the life. He who believes in Me, though he may die, he shall live. And whoever lives and believes in Me shall never die" (John 11:25–26, NKJV).

- "I am the true vine, and My Father is the vinedresser" (John 15:1, NKJV).

- "I am the way, the truth, and the life. No one comes to the Father except through Me" (John 14:6, NKJV).

And this is eternal life, that they may know You, the only true God, and Jesus Christ whom You have sent. And now, O Father, glorify Me together with Yourself, with the glory which I had with You before the world was.

—John 17:3, 5, NKJV

The prayer of Jesus Christ in His earthly body was a cry of the human soul. He was the lord of His soul, realizing the importance of His redemptive mission on Earth was an act of subjugation of the spiritual experience and fear, demonstrated by His saying, "Not My will, but Yours, be done.

—Luke 22:42, NKJV

For what the law could not do in that it was weak through the flesh, God did by sending His own Son in the likeness of sinful flesh, on account of sin: He condemned sin in the flesh, that the righteous requirement of the law might be fulfilled in us who do not walk according to the flesh but according to the Spirit. For those who live according to the flesh set their minds on the things

*of the flesh, but those who live according to the Spirit, the things of the Spirit.
For to be carnally minded is death, but to be spiritually minded is life and
peace. Because the carnal mind is enmity against God; for it is not subject to
the law of God, nor indeed can be. So then, those who are in the flesh cannot
please God.*

—Romans 8:3–8, NKJV

The Father, Son, and Holy Spirit—in one word, God—are the
totality of perfection in love for created man. In the idea of the
Creator are perfection and wisdom, to bring into reality what was
foreseen from the beginning: restoration of the relationship between God and man in the renewed covenant, where God, for his
part, gives a new birth from the word of God and the Holy Spirit,
and man, with all responsibility and consciousness of how this
forgiveness and redemption is given—at the cost of the life of the
Son of God—accepts this undeserved gift of grace with gratitude.

The one who is born again in God must grow spiritually, and
the word of God is the indispensable nourishment for the human
spiritual component—it is the truth of God proceeding from the
mouth of God, and the source, like wisdom gushing forth from the
Holy Spirit, giving revelations of the truth of God.

Newborn in Christ must grow spiritually, being transformed
into the same image of the Lord, acquiring the will and character
of Jesus Christ.

As God the Father is in unity with the Son, who is the Lord
of lords, so we are in unity with our Lord as one body in Christ
Jesus, since the Spirit of the risen Christ quickened our spirit in us
to eternal life, as one with the Son of God: "For as many as are led
by the Spirit of God, these are sons of God" (Rom. 8.14, NKJV).

But he who is joined to the Lord is one spirit with Him.
—1 Corinthians 6:17, NKJV

The victory of Jesus as a man consisted in his being in communion with the Father. Our victory over our flesh in the first place also lies in being in unity with the Lord, and his will must be a priority and not ours, as a guarantor of success: "He who overcomes shall inherit all things, and I will be his God and he shall be My son" (Rev. 21:7, NKJV).

The Word of God is a life-giving Spirit, capable of reviving the human spirit through the word of God, proceeding from the mouth of God, as vital information. This information is available to everyone who accepts this truth by faith and carries out their life path on the basis of the divine principles of righteousness, reaching that standard in communion with the Lord in the will of God, provided initially before the creation of the universe.

CHAPTER 5
WHAT IS TRUE?

What is truth?

—John 18:38, NKJV

To understand what truth is, one must refer to the original; what is the meaning of this word? The first word was spoken by God, naturally, and the meaning is embedded in this word by God himself.

First, in the material world, man, created by the Lord God, is a priority in God's plan. Second, a man made in the image of God naturally reflects the image of the Lord God. Third, man, created by God, is naturally exactly identical to the image of the Lord.

God speaks the truth to the listener in order for him to hear from the one who speaks the truth, authority, and advantage. The listener is given the right to hear and the right of dignity to remain in what he hears, and also to contain in himself what is commanded by the Lord God Himself.

The first man, created in the image of God, reflected the image provided by God from the very beginning, where the spirit, soul, and body in a person, as one organism, abided in truth, in the truth of God, having meaning in the mind and wisdom in the heart.

The Lord God put into man a feature that distinguishes him from other creation, and this feature is the conscience—a consciousness, a soul. This is what distinguishes a person from an animal, from artificial intelligence, and from angels.

Angels do not have a soul. Animals do not have intelligence and are not the image of the Lord in the trinity.

Artificial intelligence is a system, but no artificial intelligence can compete with the intelligence of God and his truth. Artificial intelligence is a system, and God's intellect is life, love, wisdom, and consciousness, and the Lord God endowed a person with these qualities, giving him the freedom to choose his thoughts and actions.

In the primordial world, a person staying in the Garden of Eden had a real natural dialogue with the Lord, able to express his thoughts in colloquial speech, in words.

The Lord God provided man with an alphabet, in which he put meaning and significance in symbolic, pictographic signs (letters).

In the original, given by the Lord God, a semantic order is embedded in the set of these symbolic signs (letters). The first two signs or letters determine the significance of the superiority of the giver to the person (alpha and beta).

Aleph is the first letter in the alphabet, and the name of God begins with the first letter. In order of priority, independence, authority, and the semantic meaning embedded in this letter as the beginning of everything, the Lord God is first: he is the path of truth and life, the Alpha.

Bet, or beta, the second letter in the alphabet, has the meaning of "home" or "dwelling place." The Lord God initially, even in this set of pictographic signs, put in the first place the basis that the Lord God created the universe, in which he wants to stay. He created for himself a sphere of dwelling in the spirit, and this sphere is the human spirit.

God is in heaven (in the spiritual sphere), and man is on earth (in the material world), but at the level of the spirit, God admonishes a person, and the whole process from the information received (revelations from God) to its implementation or fulfillment takes a certain period of time.

And in this period of time, an important role that determines the fate of a person is his consciousness. Consciousness is understanding of the will of God individually for each person, and a conscious decision is the act of faith: "Now faith is the substance of things hoped for, the evidence of things not seen" (Heb. 11:1, NKJV).

> *But without faith it is impossible to please Him, for he who comes to God must believe that He is, and that He is a rewarder of those who diligently seek Him.*
>
> —Hebrews 11:6, NKJV

He is invisible, but man must be firmly convinced and confident in God's promised true word of life, since His word is the truth.

The word truth is read "emet" and consists of three pictographic signs.

The first symbolic sign or letter, "aleph," symbolizes God the Creator as a strong God who gives life.

The second symbolic sign or letter is "mem," symbolizing an open vessel or the activity of water, like wisdom spouting from the source of the superconscious, like a source of living water, symbolizing active activity: "And He said to me, 'It is done! I am the Alpha and the Omega, the Beginning and the End. I will give of the fountain of the water of life freely to him who thirsts'" (Rev. 21:6, NKJV).

The third symbolic sign or letter is "tav." The word *truth* in the form of a cross has the meaning "new beginning." It is the triumph of victory over the law of sin and death, as confirmation of the promised justification. God is righteous as Legislator and Judge, having given mankind the gift of God (grace), acting in the life of everyone who consciously accepts and understands this truth.

Emet is spelled / emet / amet / tav /, which means "the truth is, was, and remains in eternity," and this is what God says in his word: "'I am the Alpha and the Omega, the Beginning and the End,'" says the Lord, "who is and who was and who is to come, the Almighty'" (Rev. 1:8, NKJV). And all scripture in the original God-given alphabet, from the first letter, aleph, to the last letter, tav, determines the meaning lain down by God himself from the very beginning, foreshadowing the renewal of God's relationship with man.

Calvary, the cross in the center of the earth: Jesus being crucified on this cross occupies the central part of the consciousness of all mankind. God's truth remains the truth; moreover, Christ is the life-giving Spirit in the human body of Jesus, and the identity of the Father contains the vital ability; therefore, this Spirit of life has power over death.

In the same way, the same life-giving spirit of the resurrected Jesus, as a sign of the victorious testimony in the whole universe, has power and authority in the spiritual world as the Lord of lords, the King of kings, and the perfecter of the faith of mankind: "Who for the joy that was set before Him endured the cross, despising the shame, and has sat down at the right hand of the throne of God" (Heb. 12:2, NKJV).

I am the Living One; I was dead, and now look, I am alive for ever and ever! And I hold the keys of death and Hades.

—Revelation 1:18, NIV

His name is called The Word of God.
—Revelation 19:13, NKJV

Jesus Christ is the Son of God and is the truth and life and the only way to be reborn to eternal life in the real presence of God, when the unique privilege will be given to see the Lord God as he is—and not only this, but also to be like him.

Thus, the rejection of this truth, in its irresponsibility, is that opposition of the spirit of apostasy, which was originally born in the spiritual realm, and the name of this opposition is a lie as a product of the idea of apostasy, and the fruit of this idea is death, or rejection by God and exile.

Truth appeals to reason. To everyone who has the ability to hear this day: come back, repent, and submit to live: "But do not forget this one thing, dear friends: With the Lord a day is like a thousand years, and a thousand years are like a day. The Lord is not slow in keeping his promise, as some understand slowness. Instead he is patient with you, not wanting anyone to perish, but everyone to come to repentance" (2 Pet. 3:8–9, NIV).

God has given humanity millennia, from the day of creation to the present day and to future times determined by God, but God has moments.

Humanity is essentially in the process of rehabilitation and restoration of the authority and dignity of the privileged status of the sons of God (Rom. 8:19, NKJV).

Mankind is essentially in the process of rehabilitation, and restoration of the authority and dignity of the privileged status of sons of God: "For as many as are led by the Spirit of God, they are sons of God" (Rom. 8:14, NKJV). Jesus Christ is the life-giving Spirit, the Spirit of life, the Spirit of truth, and he alone is the only way to bring about the restoration of the authority and dignity of the privileged status of the sons of God.

Jesus said: "I am the way and the truth and the life; no one comes to the Father except through Me."

—John 14:6, NKJV

KNOWING YOURSELF AND YOUR DESTINY

CHAPTER 6
MAN IS THE BUILDER OF HIS DESTINY

He who overcomes shall inherit all things, and I will be his God and he shall be My son.

—Revelation 21:7, NKJV

Let Us make man in Our image, according to Our likeness.

—Genesis 1:26, NKJV

At the very beginning, God foresaw the future, from image to likeness. Having created man in the image of God, ultimately, God foresaw the reflection of the Lord in man. In the same way as God in Himself affirmed the status of the trinity—God the Father, God the Son, God the Holy Spirit—God also established the status of trinity in mankind: spirit, soul, and body as one unity, one organism.

Jesus, who was born in a human body, lived his earthly life with dignity and is an example for all who also want to live their lives with dignity. Jesus, growing up in a family of ordinary people, was in obedience to them and in obedience all the time from infancy to adulthood.

In Nazareth, the city of His childhood and youth, Jesus grew in wisdom and stature and in favor with God and men (Luke 2:51–52, NKJV). This means the decision to be in obedience forms character, a strong-willed character capable of controlling one's feelings, desires, and emotions. First of all, God wants to see this quality in each of us.

In the spirit of the mind, ideas and desires are born, and in the depths of the soul, the heart's intentions and decisions are born. But in the end, actions are performed in the body. In the course of the life path, a lifestyle is established in accordance with one's perfect daily decisions and actions: "And the Child grew and became strong in spirit, filled with wisdom; and the grace of God was upon Him" (Luke 2:40). Already at the age of twelve, Jesus, being in the temple, amazed the teachers with his reasonable and wise answers (Luke 2:46–47, NKJV). This indicates that Jesus was an excellent student, but he grew and strengthened his spirit through direct contact with the spiritual Father at the level of the Spirit.

A person at the very beginning of his life path, growing up, needs a renewal of the spirit of the mind through the acceptance of true information—God's spoken word. Knowledge is acquired in schools, institutes, academies, and so on, but the renewal of the spirit of the mind is possible only through the acceptance of God's truth.

Jesus did not need to renew the spirit of the mind, since he was born without sin and blemish, while man at conception inherits the predominant sinful factor, established under the rule of the law of sin and death. Thus, he absorbs into himself (into his not-yet-approved mind) everything that is lain upon him from childhood.

In the process of growing one's personality, the time given by God to everyone determines the values and priorities that characterize an accomplished person of character and will, who consciously chooses his own path with all responsibility, in accordance with the formed mentality.

Jesus consciously declared his mission at the age of twelve: "I must be about My Father's business" (Luke 2:49, NKJV). But according to the established order and traditions at that time, a rabbi or a teacher could start serving when he reached a certain age.

Jesus entered the ministry at the age of thirty and remained in ministry for three and a half years, fulfilling his mission on earth exactly as the Father commanded him.

The mission of man on this Earth in the plan of God is to conform in his mind to the image of Jesus Christ: "For you must have the same mind that was also in Christ Jesus" (Phil. 2:5, NIV).

Jesus knew who he was, knew why he was on earth, and knew and realized all the responsibility as a person in making decisions, subordinating his will to obedience to the Spirit that is in Him, saying, "Not my will, but Yours, be done" (Luke 22:42, NKJV).

As a man, in an earthly human body, Jesus also had a trinity: spirit, soul, and body as one whole, a single organism. He also had feelings and emotions (he wept and rejoiced), felt pain, and experienced suffering, but he could control his emotions and focus daily on that statement—who he is and what he is for. The key to success is prayerful communication with the Father (who is in heaven in the spiritual realm, and he is Jesus at the moment on earth in the material world), and this is his victory as a man.

God has set standards, and man needs to know those standards in order to achieve what God wants. Knowledge is given by God, and its acquisition enlightens the mind and makes the heart wiser, from where all desires and their corresponding actions come from, which ultimately shapes the fate of a person.

The word *man* (human), created in the image of God and in the original, God-given language, means "Adam." The word *Adam* consists of three pictographic symbols (letters): aleph, dalet, mem.

Aleph is the first letter in the alphabet. The name of God, Elohim, also begins with the letter aleph. Thus, the meaning laid down by God is that a person is an affiliation of God. Moreover, God's Spirit, as the breath of life abiding in Adam, was a participant in divine life giving, in the very process of inhaling air: "And the LORD God formed man of the dust of the ground, and breathed into his nostrils the breath of life; and man became a living being" (Gen. 2:7, NKJV). Divine life creation means that we live while there is breath.

Dalet and mem combined mean "the activity of the blood in the body." Blood supplies the entire body with vital elements. In the blood is life for the body, and the body depends on the activity of the blood, which gives duration and function to the whole body as a whole.

Dam, or adama, means the Earth—that is, the body of organic elements that make up and determine the planet: "For dust you are, And to dust you shall return" (Gen. 3:19, NKJV).

Adam (man) is a spirit from God in an earthly body, and at his creation, Eve was in him, in Adam. "Then the rib which the LORD God had taken from man He made into a woman, and He brought her to the man" (Gen. 2:22, NKJV). In matter is the flesh of the flesh, and in the spiritual sphere is the spirit of the spirit. The first Adam became a living soul, but the Lord is a life-giving Spirit, and we were chosen in Him even before the foundation of the world: "As was the earthly man, so are those who are of the earth; and as is the heavenly man, so also are those who are of heaven" (1 Cor. 15:48, NIV).

That which is born of the flesh is flesh, and that which is born of the Spirit is spirit.

—John 3:6, NKJV

Jesus said, "You must be born again."

—John 3:7, NKJV

At the level of the spirit of the mind, this birth takes place in the mind of a person at the moment of accepting the truth. Just as a seed at the moment of conception and fertilization performs its function and a new life is born in the material world, so in the human spirit there is a renewal of the spirit of the mind in order to bring good fruits to God that are pleasing to God.

The intellectual spirit in man is an invisible component, but it is a central component in contact with the Holy Spirit: "For as many as are led by the Spirit of God, these are sons of God" (Rom. 8:14, NKJV).

There is a danger of being led by another spirit, an unclean spirit, a spirit of apostasy, rejected by God, defiled the conscious-ness of mankind, in an opposing, rebellious force and naturally bearing fruits that are displeasing to God. Man is responsible for what he chooses. The word of God is truth and life, like a seed sown by the Holy Spirit into the consciousness of man to renew the spirit of the mind, enlightening and renewing his thinking, and thereby a new creation is born in Christ Jesus, capable of bearing fruits pleasing to God in purity of conscience: "But the noble make noble plans, and by noble deeds they stand" (Isa. 32:8, NIV).

The first man was tempted by the spirit of apostasy, having accepted into his mind a seductive, doubtful thought presented in a distorted form, and at the moment of acceptance or consent, an action was performed, and the corrupt goal was achieved by the enemy. In this case, this enemy is the spirit of apostasy. He appeared to man in the form of a snake; he can also appear in the form of an angel of light: "Now the serpent was more cunning than any beast of the field which the LORD God had made. And he said to the woman, 'Has God indeed said…'" (Gen. 3:1, NKJV). This inspired doubt.

> *Then the serpent said to the woman, "You will not surely die."*
> —Genesis 3:4, NKJV

He lied and stole faith or trust in God, destroyed unity, and gave birth to self-will and the corrupt idea of independence from God. Hence all the false teachings about God, which give rise to lies: "For God knows that in the day you eat of it your eyes will be opened, and you will be like God, knowing good and evil" (Gen. 3:5, NKJV). He convinced the person as a completed act, and at that moment began the fall of man.

Ideas containing semantic meaning are born in the spirit, and information is the determining factor of meaning. What information does a person feed himself, what does he use in building his destiny, and what is the central building material—sand, strawlike garbage, or durable material like stone (truth)?

In other words: Who is the person? Who did he, in the course of his life path, grow or build from himself? Did he build his structure, his fate, on a stone (truth), or maybe his whole life flew by in a stormy gust of wind, throwing dust up and down, having no rest and shelter and constancy? Building his destiny on the sand seeping through his fingers, trying to hold on while exhausted and suffering, relying on his virtues, talents, opportunities, finances, knowledge, and strength, but in the end, unable to hold in his hands what is impossible to hold?

A man was making plans in his mind, being sure and hoping for something or someone, and suddenly something went wrong: that which he thought reliable turned out to be wrong, financial support collapsed, health was shaken, and death came when he didn't expect it at all.

The foundation, as a product of the received information in thoughts—as a spiritual component, and the foundation laid in the heart, as the heart's intentions in the soul—is a project for the implementation of the construction of the entire structure: destiny.

The formation of character and will, in the process of the entire life path, is the construction of a person in achieving the tasks and goals set by a person, and in the end, when the whole building is built into an accomplished person, God, as an Inspector, qualifies this building according to his standards.

The spirit and soul cannot be seen by the human eye; they are an invisible component in a person, but the soul depends on the spirit, because without the spirit there is no life: "For as the body without the spirit is dead, so faith without works is dead also" (James 2:26, NKJV). Man's fate is either in the works of faith or in the works of unbelief.

The soul of a person is an inner invisible person, where all the main work takes place. It is like an object or vessel or container that receives everything that comes in and processes the incoming material or information. Within, distribution and sorting take place, and information is retained or discarded, depending on the quality, and the quality is determined by the standard.

God determined the standards before the creation of the universe and put his seal and signature according to the laws established by him.

The soul of a person, and this is the will of a person, is his character, as a conductor between two powerful generators: spirit and flesh: "For the flesh desires what is contrary to the Spirit, and the Spirit what is contrary to the flesh. They are in conflict with each other, so that you are not to do whatever you want" (Gal. 5:17, NIV).

The Spirit of God is like a powerful generator, charging the human spirit with the energy of truth and renewal of the spirit of the mind, directing spiritual thoughts that can subdue emotions and will—that is, take control of the urges of sinful flesh and then, in a single stream of energy, as one whole unity, as one organism, function with dignity and quality and be blessed and pleasing to the Lord. And not only this, but also visually you can identify and distinguish a person by his deeds committed in body.

The generator of the flesh in a person prevails with a powerful influence, charging the spirit's carnal nature with emotions, feelings, and sensations, lulling the conscience, and it carries him away in the flow of energy to another sphere of spiritual manifestations and various addictions, thereby seizing the human consciousness, holding and depriving it of common sense. In the worst case, an obsession is when a person is not able to control himself, like a spiritually paralyzed disabled person. He then becomes an instrument of infamy, outrage, and madness, and you can visually determine a person by his deeds and actions committed in the body.

The flesh or body of a person cognizes the universe through hearing, sight, smell, touch, and taste. Sensation and emotional perceptions produce an effect in thinking and decision, controlling emotions.

A person who is not controlled, who does not have self-control in the spirit (obedience to the truth in righteousness), ignores the signals of conscience that warn against the influence of sensations and perceptions, due to the temptations and seductions of his own lust: "But each one is tempted when he is drawn away by his own desires and enticed; it gives birth to sin; and sin, when it is full-grown, brings forth death" (James 1:14, NKJV).

Hence from here come all the problems of mankind, all kinds of dependence—alcoholism, drug addiction, immoral sexual addiction, and all kinds of perversions—as well as informational internet addiction, which pollutes the thinking of the new generation. This is visually reflected in actions and lifestyle, in terms of values and priorities both individually and in the whole community.

A visually visible body is like the reproduction of the perception of others; it can be beautifully and elegantly adorned with outfits and jewels with professional manicures, pedicures, and makeup with exquisite taste and fragrance: "Does a young woman forget her jewelry, a bride her wedding ornaments?" (Jer. 2:32, NIV).

The visually visible body is a reflection of the internal state of the individual; at present, as indeed in the past, people are overly carried away with peculiar styles of clothing, makeup, tattoos, and piercings, losing their balance and balancing the limit of ingenuity and forgetting about who a person is and what the will of God is for a person.

At the present time, people believe that all people are equal, love is love, and a person has power over his body—it's like a repeating vicious circle, twisting into itself everyone, independent and free from divine principles and standards. In their willfulness, men want to be women by changing their gender, and women want to play the role of a husband, and with advancing technology, this is possible and accessible at the present time.

Man has a choice, but God has standards that determine the quality and purpose for application according to the law of God. According to the law of creation, everything has its purpose, in accordance with the legislative power, as a result of the transgression of the law—condemnation and, naturally, a sentence and the last word from God.

God, as the possessor of all mankind and as the supreme legislator of all created things, has the right to qualify his work: either it conforms to the standard, or it doesn't.

Humanity, which promotes its statements, beliefs, and ideas, ignoring these standards, is trying to legalize and justify its willfulness and put God in the position of the accused, without having any authority, since the legislator has a legal right.

For everything that happens on the planet Earth, humanity is fully responsible to the Creator. They are responsible for all their ideas and their implementation into reality.

With each personally, God conducts his invisible spiritual work, where the value of the individual is weighed on the scales of God, measured in the ratio of the volume of fullness and emptiness. In the book of Daniel, God showed wanting/very light in the person of the King Belshazzar.

Tekel: You have been weighed on the scales and found wanting.
—Daniel 5:27, NKJV

Any arrogance in one's own eyes before God is emptiness and nonsense: "Then this Daniel distinguished himself above the governors and satraps, because an excellent spirit was in him" (Dan. 6:3, NKJV). A lofty spirit is a void that has no meaning and value in the eyes of God. God was glorified in Daniel but blasphemed in Belshazzar.

Therefore, everyone who makes efforts in the construction of his destiny, who achieves results, is weighed on the scales of righteousness and dignity with God: "He who overcomes shall inherit all things, and I will be his God and he shall be My son" (Rev. 21:7, NKJV). And this is like the seal of God in the covenant between God and man.

Man is the builder of his own destiny and is responsible for what he chooses. Accepts or rejects the truth, acts according to Divine principles or according to the principles of this world. Will he allow God to be sealed with the Holy Spirit, as a pledge of the salvation promised by God, from the coming wrath of God? Since that impostor will appear in the future and call himself a god and put his seal and pledge for condemnation, and whatever a person chooses, he will receive, in accordance with the established mentality and established lifestyle. Time plays a huge role in the fate of a person; time flies, and it cannot be returned back. One cannot be frivolous and ignore the truth.

Chapter 6
Parallels of Human Fate

But let your "Yes" be "Yes," and your "No," "No." For whatever is more than these is from the evil one.

—Matthew 5:37, NKJV

Human consciousness is a parallel brought to life, forming destiny. The only difference is that consciously, a person draws this line or does not realize or even does not understand, but simply flows with the flow, having neither meaning nor purpose nor the final point of the life path.

In his mind, a person can be honest and dishonest or sly, and in his honesty he can honestly say either yes or no, distinguishing truth from falsehood. The evil one, if he says yes or no, then his wickedness is in his corrupt mind.

But a person does not always make the right decisions in his mind, and the consequences of the actions taken depend on this. If a sane person makes a mistake, then in his mind, he is able to judge and correct the situation, but he does this either in purity of heart or with cunning, compromising in the circumstances.

A person affirmed in the truth in his mind draws this parallel, foreseeing the final destination, and makes his life path according to a conscience that does not compromise with craftiness. And vice versa, he who does not know how he does not have balance, being thrown first into one and then into another situation, unable in his mind to draw this line of truth parallel to his fate, but twists in vanity into a vicious, repetitive, and burdensome circle.

The Holy Spirit is the seal of God in the clear consciousness, and this is the unity of spirit and mind. The seal on the right hand means the authority given by God in the power of law and dignity: "He seals the hand of every man, That all men may know His work" (Job 37:7, NKJV).

The fate of man parallels the dignity before God, as justified and sealed by him for salvation and not subject to condemnation, when the wrath of God's justice flares up on the whole universe.

The word *parallel*, from the Greek word *parallilo* means "having the same overall direction" or side by side (wiktionary.org). The parallel also means a line drawn around the earth, where the closing point is at the starting point.

Every baby born in this world has its beginning, as a starting point of the life path and the final point—the fate of a person in parallel with God or in parallel without God, either a conscious agreement with the truth and the said yes, or a conscious rejection of the truth and the said no.

A person in the material world is limited by time in space ,and time is given to a person—now in his habitat, as time flies quickly and cannot be returned back. Now, in the existing reality, first of all, a person realizes that he really exists and can definitely declare that he exists; secondly, he realizes that his existence depends on many factors and circumstances that also really exist.

The real fact is that God has declared his existence—"I AM THAT I AM"—and the natural circumstances of reality are parallel to this statement: man is, lives, breathes, and exists because God really exists. We live by it and move and have our being (Acts 17:28, NKJV).

This truth does not depend on human consciousness. Truth is and was and abides forever, but man has come and gone, and generations succeed generations in time and space. At all times and in all generations and genealogies, God has carried out his invisible work individually and personally with everyone, concluding a covenant and agreements.

Agreement, or *yes*, comes from the word *halel*, or *hallelujah*, as evidence of a conscious and sane person in securing this covenant and agreement between God and man.

Disagreement, or *no*, is the evidence of a personality that characterizes its essence—spiritual state, mental state, and carnal state— as a single organism. It is completely subject to the influence of the opposing spirit—lies.

Such a person cannot testify in his consciousness in the universe about the covenant with God = Hallelujah.

God said, "I AM WHO I AM; I am Jehovah, the Lord." This is a statement—and hallelujah! This is a legal provision and a basis and a solid foundation in building the destiny of a sane person.

The numerical sum of the pictographic signs for "I AM WHO I AM " (Ex. 3:14, NKJV) is 888. God is love, and the numerical sum of the word love is 8. God's love is infinite—infinity because God is the God of eternity.

God is an intellectual Spirit, and he is the center of digital reality, and a person only cognizes this digital reality and improves in progressive digital technologies.

God established a numerical summation corresponding to combinations of pictographic signs given to man, where each sign has its own numerical value. For example, the number 1 is assigned to the first letter in the primordial God (alphabet), and this letter is aleph, and the meaning and meaning embedded in it is that God is the one and only and independent life giving and giving life—the primary source of all that exists.

All mathematical derivatives, both negative and positive in parallels and horizontals, depending on or starting from the unit 1, or the number one.

The Bible begins with the word *God*: "In the beginning God created" (Gen. 1:1, NKJV). Here we see the significance of the word *God*, as Elohim, which begins with the letter aleph, the first letter in the alphabet, which equals 1.

In general, in this word, God put the whole meaning of his idea of creation; through the one and only—to recreate and increase your similarity to him: "revealing of the sons of God." (Rom. 8:19, NKJV).

God put significance into numbers, so from 1 to 9—real numbers and the number 9—are a completed number, and 0 is not a number in space and time, but with God everything matters, so from not having zero, God accomplishes the meaningful. If the unit 1 is a meaningful one, it attaches to itself 0, or zero, as "not having," then this is already a significant tenth of belonging to God—a tithe.

Number 7 is the divine perfection in the fullness of creation, the divine idea or will, as a result satisfying God, as self-affirmation and the basis of all foundations, as the law and seal of God. It is the truth.

Every person living here on Earth has the opportunity and chance, given by God, to be honored with the privilege of being in the truth in the body of Christ—the church and being a part of him and having the principles of dignity characteristic of him. We can be a part of his righteousness, be a part of his love, be a part of his power, be a part of his light, be a part of his mercy, be a part of his faithfulness, be a part of his eternity, and be a part of his holiness.

Allow him to be the center in life, as a core and as a pillar of the affirmation of the truth, capable of holding back raging storms and storms in all life.

Just as the Son of God subordinated his rights and dignity to the rights and dignity of the heavenly Father, so the Church of Christ (the pillar and ground of the truth)—his body, as a single organism, subordinated its rights and dignity under the head and perfecter of faith, the Lord Christ.

The number 6 is a symbol of material significance, as a subtotal of a completed action in a sign or letter /vav/. The number 600 in the sign /mem/ is a symbol of a closed vessel, as a completed activity, meaning "no longer capable of filling." Number 60, in the sign /samet/, is a symbol of a snake swallowing its tail, like a swirling circle, like spiritual paralysis, from a snakebite: "Here is wisdom. Let him who has understanding calculate the number of the beast, for it is the number of a man: His number is six hundred sixty-six" (Rev. 13:18, NKJV).

The beast depicts power predominantly over those who are not inscribed in the book of the Lamb; hence, it should be assumed that the Lamb has the predominant power and authority over the beast.

The beast is wounded in the head with a sword, but alive. The sword is the word of God, and the head of the beast, as a subject, is the center of an ideological system that originated initially in the spirit of apostasy, where Lucifer is the ancestor. This idea has been exposed and rejected by God, and in the sphere of the spirit in relation to God, it has neither power nor authority.

In the material physical world, this spirit of apostasy acts in rage, knowing its end. The goal of the beast is to put its image and its idea into the man created by God, sowing the seed of lies in the mind and occupying that central place that does not belong to it—consciousness. Thus, its goal is achieved.

The seal on the forehead means "to master the mind"; with God this is the word of God, like a double-edged sword (acting until the separation of the soul and spirit), and with the antigod or antichrist, this is the word of a lie or perverted and distorted (God's spoken word), with the aim of criminal corruption.

The seal on the right hand, as a symbol of trust and authority before God, is (in the idea of the beast) the goal and effort to deprive a person of this dignity, instilling and taking root in the inner person, copying the idea of the Creator.

Copying God the Creator, this rebellious spirit—the devil, a.k.a. Lucifer, a.k.a. the Antichrist—purposefully acts to advance his goal, mastering the mind and consciousness of mankind, transforming a person into the image of a beast and into his likeness.

The likeness of God is in the blessing of God, and the likeness of the devil is in the curse of God since the devil has already been condemned and will appear in judgment with those like him before the most high Lawgiver and Judge at the time appointed by God.

Jesus said, "And *you* shall know *the truth*, and *the truth* shall *make you free*" (John 8:32, NKJV). In other words, you will know that he is the truth and the life and the only way to salvation, and you will understand the mystery hidden from ages and generations (Col. 1:26, NKJV). This mystery is Christ is in you, the hope of glory (Col. 1:27, NKJV).

Now is the day of salvation, but what if tomorrow does not come? In what state will a person instantly appear before God? What will he provide in his justification as an accomplished person—his righteousness, his idea, his philosophy, theology, learning—all that he was proud of and what he was famous for, living in the body?

The body will change in the blink of an eye, as the person will appear before God in the spiritual sphere, but in his consciousness he will instantly determine in what state he appeared before God, how he used his God-given talents (as the meaning of life), and whether he increased in use (acquiring) or squandered, destroyed, and lost in his carelessness and laziness.

God gives a chance and opportunity to everyone, and nothing is impossible for God. He is able to free us from sinful slavery and break any bonds of dependence, but on one condition: only if a person wishes with all his mind and with all his heart to accept a God-given gift or talent, using it for the glory of God, making a covenant as a witness in the whole universe, saying yes and halle-lujah to God in the promise of a clear conscience.

In a covenant, both parties are responsible for their promise, knowing their rights and obligations; God is righteous and respon-sible in his trinity, and man is justified by God and is also respon-sible in his trinity, where the spirit, soul, and body, as a single organism in complete harmony, is subject to the will of God.

Born again from God, in the renewal of the spirit of the mind, he who knows the truth understands who he is—a new creation in Christ Jesus, reflecting as in a mirror the inner essence of Jesus, his character, and will.

There are three principles for the spirit, for the soul, and for the body, as the three components of man: first, in the intellectual spir-it, there is a beginning—thought and reflection, or a process of pro-cessing information that determines the meaning of the incoming thought. What spirit is this thought driven by? Therefore, set up your mind first to be awake in thoughts, as if protecting your head with a helmet: "And take the helmet of salvation, and the sword of the Spirit, which is the WORD OF GOD" (Eph. 6:17, NKJV).

Second, for the soul, as the heart's intentions and desires, to prevent the germination of bitter roots in the heart, therefore set up your heart to be awake in your intentions and desires, as if with a shield of faith, protecting yourself from temptation and not compromising: "Above all, taking the shield of faith with which you will be able to quench all the fiery darts of the wicked one" (Eph. 6:16, NKJV).

Third, for the body, as an opportunity and ability to manifest itself, set up your time to be awake in deeds and in deeds performed in the body, and practically this is achieved by constancy over time, when a person practically gains experience in prayer communication, and naturally and guidance and revelation from above from God for intelligent service.

Christ came to this earth with the mission of serving mankind, revealing holiness or that ideal of perfection, the word spoken with power. These deeds corresponded to what he preached, and finally, both in word and deed, he accomplished his ministry, proving and testifying throughout the universe of the triumphal victory of life over death in the power of the resurrection.

I beseech you therefore, brethren, by the mercies of God, that you present your bodies a living sacrifice, holy, acceptable to God, which is your reasonable service. And do not be conformed to this world, but be transformed by the renewing of your mind, that you may prove what is that good and acceptable and perfect will of God.

—Romans 12:1–2, NKJV

The will of God is when the Holy Spirit does what is pleasing to God in us and through us, and all glory belongs to God alone. This is the whole point of holiness: when the consciousness of a person and the actions of a person are one. Hallelujah—amen.

Prayer Is an Ability to Hear and to Be Heard

The effective, fervent prayer of a righteous man avails much.

—James 5:16, NKJV

The meaning of the word *prayer* comes from three pictographic symbols and is laid down by God Himself. The word *prayer* consists of three letters: one letter is *pei*, and two letters form *lamed*. The letter pei symbolizes the mouth, with the aim of speaking or expounding and expressing meaning to the listener.

The letter lamed, doubled, symbolizes the shepherd's staff, as confirmation of the authority of a single shepherd, whose voice distinguishes and understands his flock (the voice of authority is the Lord) and in this word, prayer, in the context of the whole word, means "to expound the meaning, to speak to the Lord and the one God, who is listening and answering prayers."

The secret of prayer dialogue is in faith and fidelity, as the key to open the door, and the effort to open the door is righteousness. Not righteousness in their own eyes, but justified by God, those who by faith accepted the fact of redemption and liberation from the sinful yoke of slavery and testify both in word and deed to their salvation: "And from the days of John the Baptist until now the kingdom of heaven suffers violence, and the violent take it by force" (Matt. 11:12, NKJV).

And Jesus also said, "the kingdom of God is within you."
—Luke 17:21, NKJV

The secret of fervent prayer is hidden in individuality, in personality, in consciousness, in the desire to be in unity with the Lord, gaining the experience of constant prayer communication and learning to hear the voice of the Lord. The fundamental factor is time.

Time given to everyone on this Earth for a purpose; it is like a God-given opportunity to sow seeds and harvest. The Lord is both the Sower and the Harvester, and the time for the harvest to ripen is like a process in the struggle between life and death: "Very truly I tell you, unless a kernel of wheat falls to the ground and dies, it remains only a single seed. But if it dies, it produces many seeds" (John 12:24, NIV).

Time used wisely is a process of collecting capital, growing rich spiritually in the inner man, where accumulated wealth is the fruit of the spirit: "But the fruit of the Spirit is love, joy, peace, long-suffering, kindness, goodness, faithfulness, gentleness, self-control. Against such there is no law. And those who are Christ's have crucified the flesh with its passions and desires" (Gal. 5:22–24, NKJV).

Time is not used wisely, as a process of an established lifestyle, formed in accordance with the mentality of a person who does not want to fight and defend divine principles, as opposed to the selfishness of the internal state of the person himself, ignoring the natural impulses of conscience.

The main time for everyone is work and rest, and this is a natural necessity for everyone, but the rest of the time, free time from work and sleep is a challenge. This is a choice for a reasonable distribution of time.

Daniel devoted time in constancy to prayer three times a day and gained the skills and experience of communicating with the Lord and the result of communication—a miraculous manifestation of divine power in the life of Daniel and those around him, and not only this, but having received a revelation from above from the Lord, he predicted about the sufferings of Christ the master in advance before all this happened at a certain time appointed by God.

Much can be said about the men of God—about Abraham, Joseph, Moses, David, Isaiah, and many personalities who pleased God, and God himself justified them. They lived by faith in expectation of the fulfillment of promises.

At one time, Jesus, as a man, needed to communicate with the heavenly Father and found time for solitude in prayer when everyone was sleeping, tired from a busy day, surrounded by many people, in constant movement.

Jesus was also tired, but his main priority was fellowship with the Father in solitude.

The meaning laid down by God himself in the word *prayer* is "to hear the Lord, to acquire this skill or experience of hearing the voice of the Holy Spirit, and to distinguish it from other voices or other spirits: "Beloved, do not believe every spirit, but test the spirits, whether they are of God; because many false prophets have gone out into the world" (1 John 4:1, NKJV).

In prayerful solitude, a person comes to know the Lord and his will. It is at these moments that knowledge comes from above, and the gift of the Holy Spirit for the reasonable service of the Holy Spirit comes through us, and this is pleasing to the Lord. Such worshippers he seeks himself, and they are able to worship him in spirit and in truth.

The Lord knows everyone: their lifestyle, the values and priorities of an individual person, everything secret in a person. All this is open before the Lord, and nothing can be hidden; nothing can be hidden from him. Therefore, an important and very first step in prayer is sincerity, honestly speaking to the Lord and revealing everything secret in order to receive forgiveness and deliverance from the burden of sin.

Second, in purity of conscience, one must say yes to the Lord as an act of faith, recognizing and affirming the Lord in oneself as one's personal savior, having given the promise of a pure conscience to remain in this covenant with the Lord, carrying out one's further life path on the divine principles of righteousness.

Further, time will show how a person fulfills his path in covenant with the Lord. Time is like a chance, like a precious opportunity for spiritual growth. By edifying oneself with the word of God and admonition from above from the Holy Spirit, a person becomes a precious vessel in the hands of God.

Prayer is a reflection of the inner essence of a person. God appreciates sincerity, honesty, and uncompromising faith or fidelity, which is determined in deeds of faith and in actions that characterize a person, the priority of which is the will of God.

Before asking, God knows what a person needs and provides in advance, but he deals with the honest according to honesty, and with the evil one according to the wickedness of man. God cannot be mocked.

Therefore, the desire to be heard by the Lord in prayers is, first of all, the desire of the Lord to be heard—he wants to be heard. He hears those who listen to him, and not only this, but he also protects them, and no one will snatch anyone out of his hands.

On his people are the seal of God and the autograph of the Holy Spirit—justified, elected, sanctified! Amen!

And I heard a loud voice from heaven saying, "Behold, the tabernacle of God is with men, and He will dwell with them, and they shall be His people. God Himself will be with them and be their God."

—Revelation 21:3, NKJV

The tabernacle is the Church of Christ—his body, his elect, washed by his blood. It is the new Jerusalem, the city: "prepared as a bride adorned for her husband" (Rev. 21:2, NKJV).

Everyone who understands this truth is a royal priesthood, a temple of the Holy Spirit living in him, who dwells in the "Holy of holies"—in the inner man, "the ark of the covenant." And as a righteous priest, moving daily along the path of life, he performs his daily service by faith, sprinkling the blood of the Lamb—the Son of God—affirming salvation and raising the censer with incense and aroma pleasant to the perception for the divine smell. This incense is the conscious prayer of the justified, and it is a key to opening heaven in anticipation of contact with reality in communion with the Holy Spirit.

The Lord God Jehovah, who creates and contains everything in the mighty power of the word and authority, approved the will of God, and only he is the savior of the souls of men. He is the King of kings and Lord of lords. He quickens the human spirit by his Spirit to abiding life, and his Spirit in us intercedes for us with groanings that cannot be expressed (Rom. 8:26, NKJV), because he knows the human spirit and desires to dwell in the tabernacle and in the Holy of Holies as full fledged and worthy of reverence, reverence, respect, and glorification.

The voice of authority is the Lord, with the power to settle matters at will, and he is who he said he is. He said "I AM THAT I AM" in the purpose and destiny of humanity.

ABOUT THE AUTHOR

L. Vesel is the mother of a large family. Like every mother, she wants to see her children succeed and tries to given them a word of wisdom according to the Word of God. In her relationship with the Lord, she has been tested many times. Through them all, the Lord gave her His promise, saying, "I will never leave you without bread and water." And He has never failed, proving that He is truly the bread of life and living water